Pebble Plus

Bilingüe/ Bilingual

Dientes sanos/Healthy Teeth

Todo sobre los dientes /
All about Teeth

por/by Mari Schuh

Traducción/Translation:
Dr. Martín Luis Guzmán Ferrer

Editor Consultor/Consulting Editor:
Dra. Gail Saunders-Smith

Consultor/Consultant:
Lori Gagliardi CDA, RDA, RDH, EdD

CAPSTONE PRESS
a capstone imprint

Pebble Plus is published by Capstone Press,
151 Good Counsel Drive, P.O. Box 669, Mankato, Minnesota 56002.
www.capstonepress.com

092009
005618CGS10

 Books published by Capstone Press are manufactured with paper
containing at least 10 percent post-consumer waste.

Library of Congress Cataloging-in-Publication Data
Schuh, Mari C., 1975–
    [All about teeth. Spanish & English]
    Todo sobre los dientes = All about teeth / por Mari Schuh.
    p. cm. — (Pebble Plus bilingüe. Dientes sanos = Pebble Plus bilingual. Healthy teeth)
    Summary: "Simple text, photographs, and diagrams present information about teeth, including how to
take care of them properly — in both English and Spanish"— Provided by publisher.
    Includes index.
    ISBN 978-1-4296-4595-9 (lib. bdg.)
    1. Teeth — Juvenile literature. I. Title. II. Title: All about teeth. III. Series.
QP88.6.S3818 2010
612.3'11 — dc22   2009040916

Editorial Credits
Sarah L. Schuette, editor; Katy Kudela, bilingual editor; Adalin Torres-Zayas, Spanish copy editor;
    Veronica Bianchini; designer and illustrator; Eric Manske and Danielle Ceminsky, production specialists

Photo Credits
Capstone Press/Karon Dubke, all

The author dedicates this book to her nephew, Alex Schuh of Tracy, Minnesota, who has 13 baby teeth.

Note to Parents and Teachers

The Dientes sanos/Healthy Teeth set supports national science standards related to
personal health. This book describes and illustrates the functions of teeth in both English
and Spanish. The images support early readers in understanding the text. The repetition
of words and phrases helps early readers learn new words. This book also introduces
early readers to subject-specific vocabulary words, which are defined in the Glossary
section. Early readers may need assistance to read some words and to use the Table of
Contents, Glossary, Internet Sites, and Index sections of the book.

Table of Contents

Tabla de contenidos

Teeth

Everyone's mouth is full of teeth. Lee started losing his baby teeth when he was 5 years old.

Los dientes

La boca de todos está llena de dientes. A Lee se le empezaron a caer los dientes cuando tenía 5 años.

Permanent teeth grew in the empty spaces. Lee will have 32 permanent teeth when he is an adult.

Los dientes permanentes crecieron en los lugares vacíos. Cuando sea adulto, Lee tendrá 32 dientes permanentes.

Parts of Teeth

Each of Lee's teeth has
its own size, shape,
and job.

Las partes de los dientes

Cada uno de los dientes de
Lee tiene su propio tamaño,
forma y función.

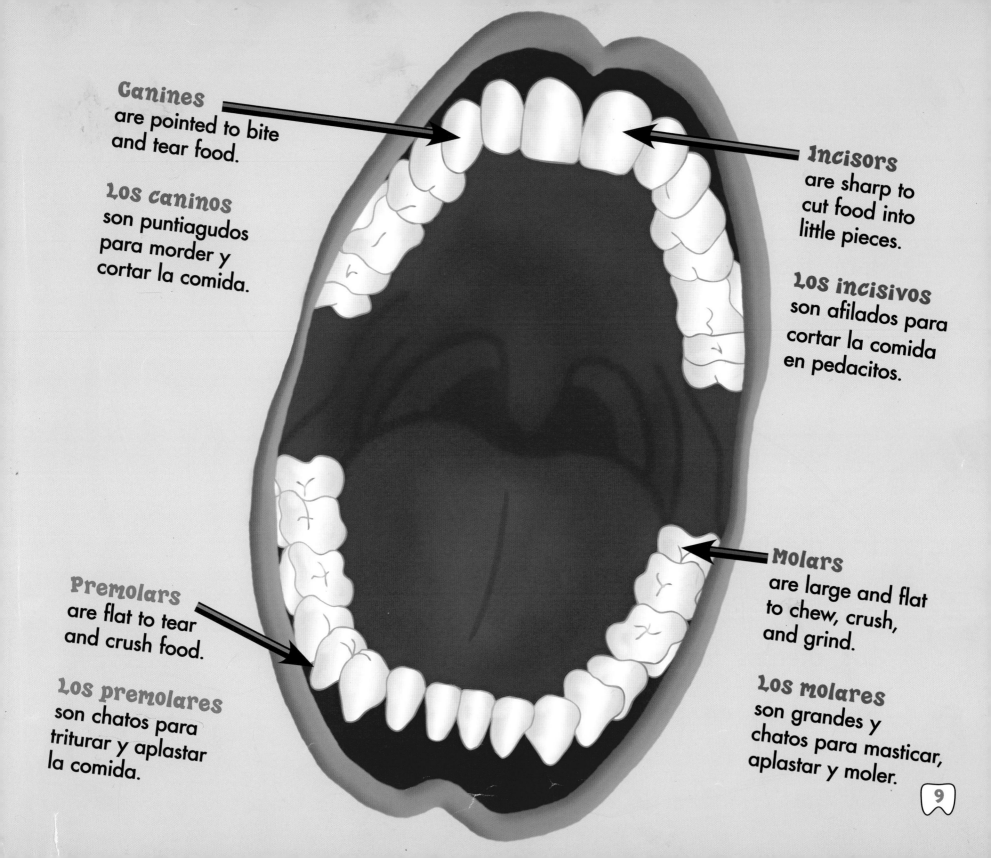

Canines are pointed to bite and tear food.

LOS CANINOS son puntiagudos para morder y cortar la comida.

Incisors are sharp to cut food into little pieces.

LOS INCISIVOS son afilados para cortar la comida en pedacitos.

Molars are large and flat to chew, crush, and grind.

LOS MOLARES son grandes y chatos para masticar, aplastar y moler.

Premolars are flat to tear and crush food.

LOS PREMOLARES son chatos para triturar y aplastar la comida.

9

Lee's sharp front teeth bite and tear food. His wide back teeth mash food into small pieces.

Los dientes frontales afilados de Lee muerden y cortan la comida. Los dientes traseros anchos muelen la comida en pedacitos.

The crown is the part you can see.

Strong enamel covers the crown.

Roots hold the teeth into the gums.

La corona es la parte del diente que puedes ver. Un esmalte fuerte cubre la corona. Las raíces mantienen fijos los dientes en las encías.

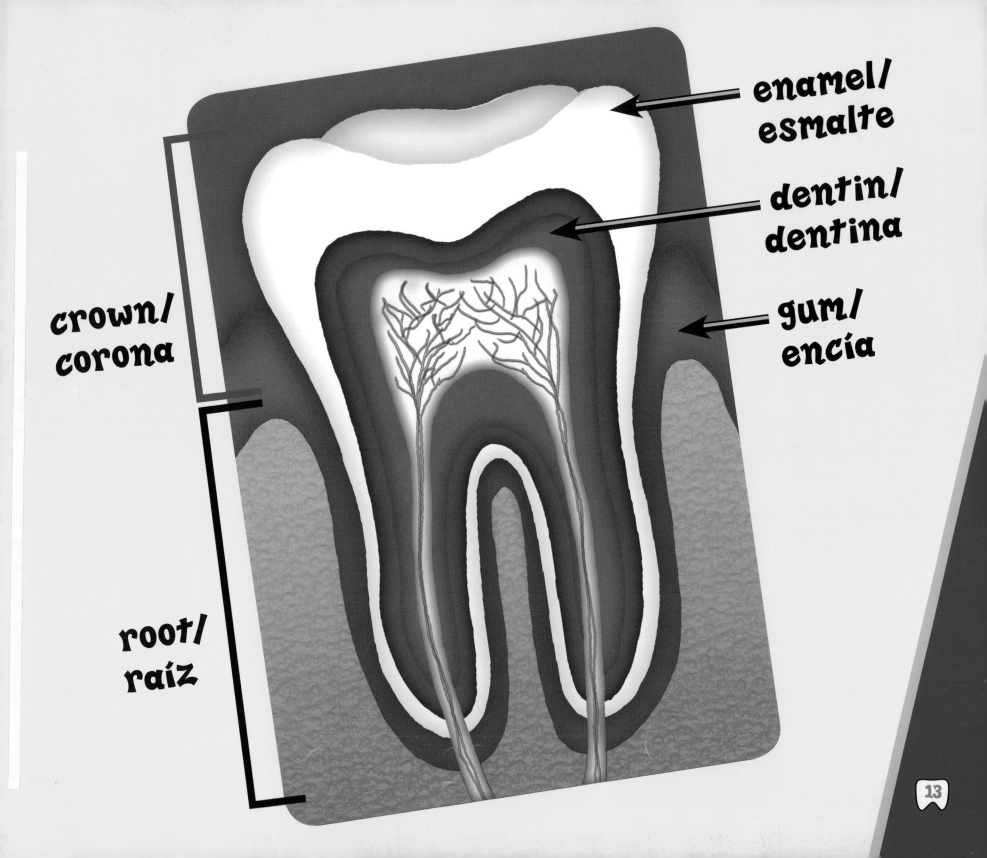

enamel/
esmalte

dentin/
dentina

gum/
encía

crown/
corona

root/
raíz

13

Healthy Teeth

Lee knows that eating too many sweets can give him cavities. He brushes his teeth at least twice every day.

Dientes sanos

Lee sabe que si come muchos dulces esto puede causarle caries. Él se cepilla los dientes por lo menos dos veces al día.

Food gets stuck between Lee's teeth. He flosses every day to keep his teeth and gums healthy.

La comida se queda atorada en los dientes de Lee. Él usa el hilo dental todos los días para mantener sus dientes y encías sanos.

Lee visits the dentist's office twice
a year. His teeth are cleaned
and checked for cavities.

Lee va al consultorio del dentista dos
veces al año. Le limpian los dientes
y examinan que no tengan caries.

Smile!

You should take care of your teeth too. You will have a healthy smile your whole life!

¡Sonríe!

Tú también debes cuidar tus dientes. ¡Así tendrás una sonrisa sana toda tu vida!

Glossary

baby teeth — a child's first set of teeth; children have 20 baby teeth; baby teeth are also called primary teeth.

cavity — a decayed part or hole in a tooth

crown — the top part of a tooth that you can see

enamel — the hard, glossy covering on teeth; enamel protects teeth from decay.

gum — the firm skin around the base of teeth

permanent teeth — the teeth you have your whole life; most people have 32 permanent teeth.

root — the part of a tooth that holds it in the mouth; roots are found inside your gums.

Internet Sites

FactHound offers a safe, fun way to find Internet sites related to this book. All of the sites on FactHound have been researched by our staff.

Here's all you do:

Visit *www.facthound.com*

FactHound will fetch the best sites for you!

Glosario

la carie — parte carcomida o agujero en el diente

la corona — la parte superior del diente que puedes ver

los dientes de leche — primer juego de dientes del niño; los niños tiene 20 dientes de leche; los dientes de leche también se llaman dientes primerizos.

los dientes permanentes — los dientes para toda tu vida; la mayoría de las personas tienen 32 dientes permanentes.

la encía — piel firme que rodea la base del diente

el esmalte — la cubierta dura y brillosa que cubre al diente; el esmalte protege a los dientes de deterioro.

la raíz — parte del diente que lo sostiene en la boca; las raíces están dentro de tus encías.

Sitios de Internet

FactHound brinda una forma segura y divertida de encontrar sitios de Internet relacionados con este libro. Todos los sitios en FactHound han sido investigados por nuestro personal.

Esto es todo lo que tú necesitas hacer:

Visita *www.facthound.com*

¡FactHound buscará los mejores sitios para ti!

Index

Índice